BLUFF YOUR WAY IN BASEBALL

Jerry Bobrow,
R.B.I., M.V.P., D.H.

CENTENNIAL PRESS

Having been the only kid west of the Mississippi not to make a Little League All-Star team, I devoted the next 30 years of my life to finding out why. It's this quest that endeared the great game of baseball to me and propelled me through many years of playing, bench warming, scorekeeping, bench warming, announcing, bench warming, coaching, bench warming, umpiring, bench warming, and warming the bench. Some players dream of the pros; I dream of Little League All-Stars. So when the opportunity arose for me to write a book on baseball – the offer was sent to me by mistake (wrong name and address) – I seized the moment and changed my name. I did, however, need the consulting, researching, and editing assistance of people who knew something about the great game. Unable to find any, I settled for unverified information and rumors from over-the-hill softball star Marty Heisey and former crooked-arm fireballer Steve ("Ya can't hit what ya can't reach") Hariton. The creative consulting was done by baseball card afficionado Peter Z Orton, who is still saving for a 1956 mint Mantle. Now, with my credentials squarely on the table, let's bluff.

WARNING: Sometimes fact is stranger than fiction. Hard as it may be to believe, 97.3% of this book is accurate, factual information, 2.6% is slightly exaggerated for interest's sake, and .1% is absolute nonsense.

ISBN 0-8220-2202-8
© Copyright 1990 by Centennial Press

Printed in U.S.A.
All Rights Reserved

Centennial Press, Box 82087, Lincoln, Nebraska 68501
an imprint of Cliffs Notes, Inc.

INTRODUCTION

The life of a baseball bluffer can be interesting and challenging, yet fraught with danger. Tinkering with baseball knowledge is like fooling with mother nature; be careful – one false move and the finely balanced ecology is gone. On the other hand, a successful baseball bluff is unparalleled in satisfaction. Being able to go home and look in the mirror and say, "I can't believe it, it worked! They're calling me the Carl Sagan of the baseball world!" is worth every anxiety-filled moment. Remember, the more you bluff, the more relaxed you'll feel making up information, spouting worthless trivia, and being misinformed.

Let's start with the basics and work backwards. Before you start bluffing, keep in mind

Who

Who are you trying to bluff? Friends, relatives, strangers, the boss, people you want to impress, people you want to depress? Just anyone? Be careful how you select your target. The most unathletic-looking dolt could be a mountain of baseball knowledge (and usually is).

Before you bluff, eavesdrop. If your target group is discussing the latest *Baseball Digest* or box score, look elsewhere. Listen for telltale words like "arbee-eyes," "dingers," and "heat." If you hear the word "sabre," they're probably not talking about sword fighting since SABR

3

stands for the Society for American Baseball Research, or if you hear the word "Rotisserie," they're not referring to broiling chickens but to a popular fantasy baseball league where fans select players and follow their performance closely throughout the season. Don't bluff in this crowd; they'll break your thumbs.

A safe bet as bluffee is anyone in the stands waving a pennant, wearing a baseball glove, or eating sushi. Watch for the giveaway signs of a novice: wearing a new baseball hat or funny mouse ears, sitting facing the men's room, or cheering the grounds crew. Remember that the knowledgeable baseball fan will come to the ballpark with a small radio, an old hat with lots of obscure baseball pins, several sets of binoculars, a portable vibrating cushion, and his own thick, season-long scorebook. Don't mess with this fan; he's serious business.

What

What to bluff? Since baseball's been around so long, you're probably better off bluffing about the early years of baseball and only gradually, if at all, working your way to modern times. That is, unless the person you're trying to bluff looks like he's been around since early times – in which case, the rookie prospects of Tacoma's double-A minor league club are your topic of the day.

When

Good bluffing, like good sex, is good anytime. So bluff whenever you're so moved. Probably the best time to bluff baseball is late at night or at the end of the day when bluffees aren't quite as sharp. Or after good sex.

Where

A good baseball bluff is satisfying almost anywhere – at parties, weddings, bar mitzvahs, at the local drugstore, at work, at the ballpark, or at your local sports bar where all the so-called jocks and know-it-alls hang out. We recommend bluffing only in small crowds; try to avoid national television (unlike the Al Campanis foot-swallowing incident). Be cautious when bluffing at work; remember, you'll see these people again after they've had a chance to look it up. And a few words of warning about bluffing at the ballpark: if you're sitting in the cheap seats (bleachers), don't bluff – they're the true fans' natural habitat. You're much safer bluffing in the expensive season box seats, since these fans were given tickets to grease the wheels for a big business deal. The clods in the boxes don't know spit about baseball.

Why

Why bluff baseball? Because it's there. Because baseball is the national pastime. Because it's popular, hip, and can help you become the life of the party and make new friends. Because people will think you were once a jock. Because it'll help our book sales.

How

Read this guide. Make up stuff. Mumble a lot.

Now proceed to the next page, take a deep breath, and read carefully. We'll start at the beginning. Where else?

A VERY, VERY, EXTREMELY ABBREVIATED HISTORY OF THE GAME

The most ardent baseball fan can't know everything about the 100-odd years of the game. So exhibiting esoteric knowledge of baseball's history will usually put Mr. Know-it-all in his place. What follows is a brief account of the history of the great game of baseball. But before you begin, here are a few guidelines for history bluffing:

- **Early History**—In any discussion about baseball's early history, don't hesitate to make up facts. Randomly toss in the names Ruth, Gehrig, Cobb, Tris Speaker, Cy Young, Christy Mathewson, Honus Wagner, Grover Cleveland Alexander, and Robert Redford. These names will be the answers to most questions.
- **Modern History**—In a discussion of modern history, the names Willie Mays, Mickey Mantle, Hank Aaron, Ted Williams, Stan Musial, Joe DiMaggio, Yogi Berra, Sandy Koufax, Warren Spahn, Ernie Banks, Eddie Mathews, Duke Snider, Al Kaline, and Whitey Ford are the beginning of a long, impossible-to-please-everyone list. In a pinch, throw out these names and mumble a lot.
- **Present-Day**—In any discussion about present-

day ballplayers, if in doubt, bring up the name George Steinbrenner, and the conversation will immediately take on a completely different tone. Leave as soon as punches are thrown.

Now, on with the history . . .

In the Beginning

Although Abner Doubleday is usually given credit for inventing the game, baseball can be traced as far back as Egypt in October, 3022 B.C. Early Egyptian priests participated in this contest using a melon and a shepherd's staff. Had the Egyptians further refined the sport, taverns throughout America would now be tuning in to *Thursday Night Melonball.*

Early carvings on the tomb of Beni Hasan showed half-naked women playing baseball following agricultural fertility rituals. Obviously, the game was not as popular as the rituals, and so the Pharoahs, in their wisdom, decided to keep the rituals and send baseball to Europe.

The Europeans quickly incorporated the game into their Christian ceremonies. This may be one reason that baseball is thought of by many as a religion. The English adopted the game and with slight modification called it stoolball, using milking stools as bases. Collecting stoolball cards didn't catch on, so eventually the name was changed to goal ball, then rounders, and finally, for some strange reason, baseball. Having thoroughly covered over 4000 years in three paragraphs, we now move on to the early years.

The Early Years

Although many Californians argue that American baseball didn't really begin until 1958 when the Dodgers and Giants moved to California, official records show that English immigrants brought the game of rounders to the United States in the early 1800s. Dr. Oliver Wendell Holmes reported playing the game in 1829 while at Harvard University, but no record of the opposing team or final score has ever turned up, indicating that Harvard probably lost.

At this time, baseball was a game for those of high social standing, so some standard rules had to be devised for the game to appeal to the masses (and to keep those of high social standing from beating each other senseless). In 1845, a bewhiskered surveyor named Alexander Joy Cartwright was drafted to draft rules and set upon to set standards. Cartwright proposed a regular organization and formed the first formal ball club. Fortunately, Cartwright, a surveyor used to measuring flat land, exercised excellent judgment in laying out a flat playing field. Otherwise our national pastime might have been called mountainball. Or golf.

Probably the most significant rule of Cartwright's new game provided that a player could be tagged or forced out instead of being thrown at. Up to this time, the most popular way to get a batter or runner out was to nail him with the thrown ball. This change significantly lengthened the life spans of many ballplayers. Sign-ups for teams increased dramatically. Cartwright's rules also stipulated three strikes to a batter, three outs to a side, and 90 feet between bases.

Cartwright's rules even provided for a scapegoat to

be yelled at during emotional times in a game. Hence the first umpire was created. Finally Cartwright required all team players to wear uniforms. Rumor has it that Cartwright's brother was in the clothing business and had just gotten a deal on 60,000 pairs of irregular knickers and blemished socks with no heels. Today, many famous players still express relief that the sale wasn't on hoop skirts and silk hose.

The First Recorded Game

The first recorded game in history (although all the teams were still amateur) was scheduled on June 19, 1846, when the elegant, high-class New York Knickerbockers were challenged by a group of rowdies called the New York Nine. The bet was for dinner, drinks, and dancing. The Knickerbockers had no concept of what hunger could do to motivate a ball club (although Charles Comiskey, owner of the 1919 White Sox/Black Sox, later used the same psychology). The Knicks were beaten 23 to 1 in just four innings. Barbershop pundits have been known to swear that this is also the origin of 90 percent of modern sportscasters' vocabulary ("slaughtered," "wiped out," "massacred," "devoured," "flagellated," etc.) as well as the rule to stop merciless beatings, called euthanasia.

Although the Knickerbockers wisely decided to take a five-year off-season, Cartwright's rules were universally adopted and hundreds of teams started springing up. In May of 1857, the Knickerbockers, finally recovered, called for a convention in New York to formalize the rules and some say to squelch rumors that they were planning to join the National Basketball Association. The next convention, in March of 1858, saw the organization of the first league, the National Association of Base Ball Players. They also decided to change the game to nine innings instead of "21 runs win the game." (The National Ping-Pong Association immediately adopted the 21-point system, dropping their 9-inning rule.)

First Overpriced Game

On July 20, 1858, for the first time an admission fee (50¢) was charged for a game between the teams from Brooklyn and New York. A half-hour later, the fine art of sneaking into ballparks was perfected, although the perpetrator was never found. Also originating in these years were counterfeiting tickets and scalping (selling tickets for hundreds of times their actual worth, now a vital part of the twentieth-century American economy). A hundred years later, these two cities were still trying to determine who had the best team, the most vocal fans, and the most ruthless scalpers.

More Growth

The next 50 years witnessed an incredible growth and interest in the game. But the gentlemen's game of baseball was losing its air of good sportsmanship. Yelling and screaming could be heard from the dugouts and bleachers. Baseball was developing its own brand of profanity. Gambling, bribery (now called bonus incentives), players jumping teams (now called free agency), rowdyism (still called rowdyism), and unwashed uniforms became commonplace. The stage was set . . .

Birth of the National League

Time was ripe for the birth of the National League and the coin-operated laundromat. In 1876, the National League (NL) came into existence. The COL (coin-operated laundromat) had to wait its turn.

Credit for forming the National League (originally National League of Professional Base Ball Clubs, or NLPBBC, or NL) is given to William Ambrose Hulbert, a Chicago businessman and president of the Chicago White Stockings. The name National League was chosen because the William League, Ambrose League, or Hulbert League just didn't sound strong enough to put order back into the gentlemanly game.

Assisting Hulbert in forming the NLPBBC was Boston's star pitcher, Al Spalding—the same Spalding who later founded a sporting goods manufacturing company. The story goes that during a game one particularly cold morning, Spalding was ridiculed for wearing mittens. But after he caught an exceptionally hard hit line drive without the usual shriek of pain, other players clamored to borrow Spalding's mitts. Realizing that renting mittens would entail mountains of paperwork . . . you can take it from there.

The new league constitution forbade the drinking of alcohol and gambling at games. (Yelling and screaming at the umpire were nearly outlawed until calmer heads prevailed and this was allowed—but not encouraged until the 1950s.) Baseball playing was again becoming honorable, respectable, and profitable.

In 1883, pitchers began throwing overhand. (In protest, the National Bowling League started throwing underhand.) And although everyone seemed to be throwing the ball harder, Charles "Kid" Nichols pitched a decade of games using an almost unhittable slow ball, referred to by hitters as the "butterfly," the "change of pace," or that "#%&*!*# pitch." From 1890 to 1899, Nichols won 27, 30, 35, 33, 32, 30, 30, 29, and 21 games respectively. But better known than Nichols was another outstanding pitcher, Denton True Young, nicknamed "Cy" for "Cyclone" because of his blazing fastball. Young's records include completing 758 games in 816 starts. It appears that the fine art of relief pitching had not yet been discovered.

But with the help of some outstanding ballplayers including Adrian "Cap" Anson, John J. McGraw, and Willie Henry ("Wee Willie") Keeler, baseball began to use "scientific" methods to improve the game. Unorthodox practices such as throwing the ball to your own player (called "teamwork") became popular. Backing up throws, the hit-and-run, and the bunt brought strategy to the game. One of McGraw's innovations consisted of grabbing on to the opposing runner's belt as he tried to advance to the next base. Such scientific advances greatly enhanced the sport's sophistication. But still no relief pitchers.

Birth of the American League

Although the National League (also called the Senior Circuit) was the only professional baseball league, others had different ideas. Why should anyone have a monopoly on rowdyism? So in 1901, former player and manager Charlie Comiskey and sportswriter Ban Johnson (often confused with Ben Johnson), in the American spirit of fair play and healthy competition, helped form the American League (Junior Circuit). Many famous players and managers, including

Napoleon "Nap" Lajoie, Cy Young, and Cornelius "Slats" McGillicuddy (also known as Connie Mack), quickly jumped to the new league which just happened to offer more money and bigger kickbacks.

A few years later, these two leagues—once fierce competitors—showed the great spirit of compromise and joined into the two-league Major League Baseball system. Now with mutual rowdyism and universal umpire harassment, we enter the modern era.

The Twentieth Century

There's only so much modern baseball history that any human can (or wants to) remember. So a good bluffer is selective both in what he chooses to memorize and what he chooses to fabricate. Since modern baseball history is virtually impossible to condense without sounding like a Cliffs Notes, here's a bird's-eye view. Select as you need to, improvise as you need to, but most of all, when in doubt, mumble as you need to.

The Beginning of the Modern Era

The legendary Tyrus Raymond "Ty" Cobb (the "Georgia Peach," known for sharpening his spikes before each game) is the greatest and most feared (and hated) competitor. The Peach's aggressive play convinces everyone that baseball is serious business, not child's play. Local hospital revenue is up 40 percent.

Giant manager John J. McGraw refuses to play the Boston Somersets in the 1904 World Series because of a personal feud with Boston's owner, Ban Johnson. (Can you imagine the millions of bucks the TV networks would have dropped if the Dodgers had refused to play the Athletics in the 1988 Series? It'd bankrupt Donald Trump.) After this fine display of sportsmanship, a new rule forces pennant-winning teams to play in the World Series regardless of personal squabbles, fear of losing, or Vegas odds. A few years later, a rule is designed to force players to try their hardest in the Series. Boy, tough rules!

These early years of the modern era also feature a real advance in the scientific style of play, which is dominated by the pitching of the immortal Christy Mathewson (who was not actually immortal and did, in fact, finally bite the dust), the previously mentioned legendary hitting, running, base stealing, and general mayhem of Ty Cobb, and the amazing fielding and hitting of the "Flying Dutchman," Honus Wagner. Pitching stars Mathewson, Gettysburg Eddie Plank, Mordecai "Three-Finger" Brown, John Dwight "Happy Jack" Chesbro (you'd be happy too if you won 41 games in 1904, or in any year for that matter), "Iron Man" Joseph McGinnity, Cy Young, and George Edward "Rube" Waddell (who struck out 343 batters in 1904, not all in one game) dominate the sport until 1909.

Dead-Ball Era

Baseball played during the years 1900 to 1920 is later to be known as the "dead-ball era," since the maximum flight of a baseball is about 30 feet with a tailwind. Home runs are no longer written in the box scores; they're etched in stone. In 1914, Frank "Home Run" Baker leads the American League with nine home runs. Many observers give credence to the rumor that goose-down is used in the baseballs. Taking advantage of the dead ball is the double play combination of second baseman Johnny Evers, shortstop Joe Tinker, and manager/first baseman, Frank Chance. This trio leads the Chicago Cubs to World Series championships and is immortalized in the oft-repeated poem "Tinker to Evers to Chance." Pitcher Walter Johnson averages over 26 wins per season for 10 seasons, and hurler Ed Walsh perfects the spitball and wins 40 games in a season. Batting goggles become the vogue. Hitters complain that hitting wet goosedown is a waste of energy.

The dead-ball era ends with the Black Sox Scandal of 1919. For those bluffers who haven't seen the film *Eight Men Out,* the Black Sox Scandal can be described as a semicomic effort of the underpaid Chicago White Sox of penny-pinching owner Charlie Comiskey attempting to throw the World Series to the Cincinnati Reds who can barely catch it, since Comiskey's team has all the talent (but little money, since Comiskey wants it all for himself). The splendid, talent-rich White Sox (turned Black Sox) throw the Series, depriving fans from witnessing the greatest barefoot ballplayer ever, "Shoeless Joe" Jackson, one of the eight suspended for life from baseball. (Note: He really played barefooted only once, for three innings.) Although the White Sox/Black Sox are found not guilty in court, the new and first-ever Commissioner of Baseball, iron-fisted Judge Kenesaw Mountain Landis, hired to clean up baseball, suspends the famous eight for life. The origin of the phrases "drop in the bucket" and "swept under the rug" is often attributed to these suspensions, as over 40 other well-known baseball players are also accused of similar charges without paying the piper. They'd never have escaped Judge Wapner's gavel.

Live-Ball Era

This new commissioner with the funny name is hired to usher in a new, cleaner era. And so he does. But the era from 1920 to 1930 is really known as the "live-ball era." With a new baseball that actually bounces when dropped on asphalt, the stage is set for the Big Bang style of ball, led by free-swinging and free-spirited legend Babe Ruth. Ruth's 54 home runs in 1921 not only lead the league, but are more than the entire league produced in the last umpteen years. Pitchers and low-flying birds have nervous breakdowns as the lively ball soars to new heights. Baseballs are also replaced more often and more quickly: New balls are brought into play immediately whenever one is scuffed, hit out of play, in the air, on the ground, or will not pass the white glove dust test. Baseball manufacturers are overjoyed with the new procedures and produce balls that are squeaky clean but show fingerprints.

Baseball of the Roaring 20s sees the beginning of a Yankee dynasty that produces the greatest team ever, the 1927 N.Y. Yankees' "Murderers' Row": Babe Ruth, Lou Gehrig, Bob Meusel, and Tony Lazzeri, all magnificent hitters—information vital to any bluffer because 70 percent of the baseball discussions that end in brawls start over which team was the greatest ever.

These years witness the remarkable hitting prowess of Rogers Hornsby and Harry "Slug" Heilman. Unfortunately we don't remember exactly what they did that was so remarkable. They probably each batted a mere .400 or .500 for a bunch of years.

The 30s and 40s

The antics of the St. Louis Cardinals' Gas House

Gang are led by 12 batters hitting over .300 (only nine could play at a time) and pitchers (ready for this?) Dizzy and Daffy Dean. Or was it Lumpy and Goofy? Anyway, now comes the emergence of sluggers Ted Williams, Joe DiMaggio, Stan Musial, Hank Greenberg, fireballer Bob "Rapid Robert" Feller, and the unforgettable discovery of a pitch that soon would become the basis for a league and a different form of baseball that would sweep the nation: the "eephus" pitch, thrown (or should we say blooped) by Tiger pitcher Rip Sewell. It's the forerunner of slow-pitch, high-arc softball. For those of you interested, "eephus" doesn't come from any language known to man, and people will think you're kidding when you mention it.

The first major league night games (with lights) are played in the 1930s. One such game is at Ebbetts Field in Brooklyn between the Dodgers and the Cincinnati Reds. Unfortunately, the Dodgers have night blindness as they are no-hit by pitcher Johnny Vander Meer. Since the Dodgers hit about the same in the daylight, glasses and carrot juice are ruled out as remedies.

Present-Day Era

With many players on active duty in World War II, baseball actually becomes of secondary importance for awhile. But after the war, we enter the "Big-Bucks" era, with baseball becoming a financial institution because of the popularity of the game and the sagging value of the dollar in Europe. This boom is aided by the move west of the Giants and Dodgers, billions of dollars in television and TV commercials, the players' strike of 1981, and the invention of the player's agent.

Salaries start to creep up. Everyone is called a star,

so new terms appear such as superstar, super superstar, superduper star, superduper superstar, and asteroid. You can't tell the superstar from the superduper star without a gold-embossed program.

This era is filled with about 10 million incredible, unforgettable moments. But remember that unforgettable moments to one team are moments that beg to be forgotten by the other team and their fans. Don Larsen's perfect game against the Brooklyn Dodgers in the 1956 World Series is an unforgettable moment for all Yankee fans and most of the civilized world, but ask a Dodger fan and it never happened.

So the bluffer would be wise to stay away from the present-day era of baseball. Aside from fans' selective memory, this area is fraught with pitfalls, as most Americans know more about their city's ball club (if they're winning) than about their own congressional representatives, or their own spouses for that matter.

It's best to select a few bits of minutia – so trivial that no one can argue, since no one will care. For example

Early Minutiae

- The pennant-winning Chicago Cubs won 21 games in a row in September 1935.
- Babe Ruth stole second and third base in the same inning in a 1921 World Series game (before he perfected his home run trot).
- The World Champion 1934 Cardinals – known as the Gashouse Gang – later formed a hillbilly band called the Mississippi Mudcats.

More Recent Minutiae

- Roger Craig, after losing 24 games for the New

York Mets, changed his uniform number to 13 to alter his luck and proceeded to lose only 22 games the next season.

- Al Benton was the only pitcher ever to face Babe Ruth and Mickey Mantle in regular-season American League competition. (He later recommended catcher's masks and chest protectors for pitchers.)
- Joe Pignatano hit into a triple play in his last at-bat in the major leagues (the origin of the phrase "going out in style").
- With his Cubs down by nine runs, manager Charlie Grimm, coaching at third base, dug a hole and buried his lineup card. (It was said he was trying to tunnel back to the clubhouse.)
- Greg Harris of the Phillies can pitch with both hands. Teammate Randy Ready says Harris is amphibious. (We guess he's the first pitcher who can pitch underwater.)

And finally, remember that any discussion of present-day baseball will almost certainly address Nolan Ryan, Pete Rose, Jose Canseco, Wade Boggs, Mike Schmidt, Don Mattingly, Robin Yount, Jim Abbott, Bo Jackson, George Steinbrenner, any local wonderboy, and three important phenomena: expansion, the designated hitter, and the wave (unexplainable fan reaction of standing up and sitting down in some sort of concerted unity). Since you can't know everything and you can't do anything about the last three phenomena, don't concern yourself. Just drop your few lines and leave this conversation with "Everybody thinks he's an expert!"

THE TEAMS AND
THEIR BALLPARKS

The Teams

The true baseball bluffer will know one obscure and irrelevant fact about every team—a fact that's so irrefutable and insignificant that it brings the conversation to a smashing standstill, as others can do nothing else but stare blankly or nod knowingly. More important, however, remember that when referring to a team, never, *never* use its real name. Always use the team's nickname. For example, if you refer to the Baltimore Orioles as the Orioles, you'll immediately be spotted as a baseball novice or a member of the Audubon Society. Instead, call them the O's, or the Orange Birds, or if you're at a loss for a name, use something unusual and short, such as, say, the "Balties." But whatever nickname you invent, say it with a tone of endearment and familiarity as if you've been using it for decades. Soon your more insecure friends and relatives will adopt this ridiculous tag you just coined, as if they too have been using it since childhood. What a gas, huh? Keep in mind that when you refer to teams from the east coast, always say "dem" instead of "them" as in "dem Yanks" or "da" instead of "the" as in "da Bums" (da now-defunct Brooklyn Dawdgers). You should write the following list of teams, common (and not so common) nicknames, and ballpark names and capacities on a very, very long shirt sleeve for easy reference during any baseball discussion.

National League

Atlanta Braves—*America's Team, Ted's Team,* (for owner Ted Turner); Atlanta-Fulton County Stadium, 52,003, where mascot Chief Noc-a-homa stayed in a left-field tepee until a rare Braves' home run would bring him out for a war dance.

Chicago Cubs—*Chi-Cubs, Cubbies;* Wrigley Field, 38,143, with ivy-covered outfield walls; a traditional flag flies from the top of the scoreboard after each game: blue with *W* for win, or white with *L* for loss.

Cincinnati Redlegs—*Reds, Pete's Boys, Big Red Machine;* Riverfront Stadium, 52,392, uses the original home plate from the Reds' former home, Crosley Field.

Houston Astros—*Stros, Asts;* Astrodome, 45,011, first domed baseball field.

Los Angeles Dodgers—*Blue Crew, Tommy's Gang;* Dodger Stadium, 56,000, with six tiers of seats, dubbed the "Taj Mahal of baseball."

Montreal Expos—*Spoes;* Olympic Stadium, 59,123.

New York Mets—*Da Metz;* Shea Stadium, 55,601.

Philadelphia Phillies—*Da Phils;* Veteran's Stadium, 62,382.

Pittsburgh Pirates—*Bucs, Buccos;* Three Rivers Stadium, 58,722.

St. Louis Cardinals—*Red Birds, Cards;* Busch Stadium, 53,138 semi-inebriated fans.

San Diego Padres—*Pads;* Jack Murphy Stadium, 59,022 including early Charger and chicken fans. (For the past few years the Pads have been better known for their mascot than their ballplaying.)

San Francisco Giants — *Jints, Mesomorphs;* Candlestick Park, 59,091 windblown fans.

American League

Baltimore Orioles — *O's, Da Birds, Orange Birds;* Memorial Stadium, 54,017.

Boston Red Sox — *Bosox, Hose, Dark Hose, Heartbreakers;* Fenway Park, 33,379.

California Angels — *Halos;* Anaheim Stadium, 64,573.

Chicago White Sox — *Pale Hose, Chisox;* Comiskey Park, 44,492.

Cleveland Indians — *The Tribe;* Cleveland Stadium, 77,797.

Detroit Tigers — *Bengals, Sparky's Boys* (for Sparky Anderson); Tiger Stadium, 54,220 growling fans.

Kansas City Royals — *Kaycees;* Royals Stadium, 40,762.

Milwaukee Brewers — *Brewskies, Brew Crew;* County Stadium, 46,625, where Harvey Haddix pitched 12 perfect innings and lost.

Minnesota Twins — *Twinks, Twinkies, Twinnies, Minnies;* Hubert H. Humphrey Metrodome, 55,244.

New York Yankees — *Dem Yanks, Bronx Zoo, Dem *#%*#s!;* Yankee Stadium, 57,545 angry fans.

Oakland Athletics — *A's, Swingin A's, Mustache Brigade* (when owner Charles Finley paid players to wear mustaches); Oakland Coliseum, 48,621.

Seattle Mariners — *Mares, 'Ners;* The Kingdome, 59,059.

Texas Rangers — *Strangers;* Arlington Stadium, 35,698 (an estimate, since the stadium, due to past seasons' teams, has never been filled to capacity).

Toronto Blue Jays –*Jays;* Sky Dome, recently completed, still counting the seats, presently at 54,000.

More About the Ballparks

In the early years, since teams and franchises shifted from day to day, most teams didn't have a permanent home field. But once teams became settled and remained in a city for more than a week, they quickly realized the tremendous "home-field advantage" potential. Soon every team wanted its own ballpark to suit the particular style of its players. If you had a team that always hit short fly balls to right field, you moved in the right field fence to 170 feet away and immediately had a power-studded lineup of right field bombers. Or if you had a sluggish team, you mixed beach sand in the base paths to slow everyone down to your speed. You could manipulate the field, the length of the grass, or the height of the mound. Knowing the opposing pitcher is afraid of heights, you simply added three feet of dirt to the mound the morning of the game and waited for the nosebleeds. You could also entice the crowd to cheer for your team and boo the other team (instead of booing just the umpire) by adding a behavior-modification scoreboard. And most important, by owning your own ballpark, you could make a fortune selling peanuts, hotdogs, soft drinks, beer, souvenirs, and other exorbitantly priced items.

The older stadiums ("stadia" for the literate) came in all shapes and sizes, but the more modern ones have standardized some of the important items, like beer cup size, distance to the restrooms, and the number of people per seat. The modern ballparks introduced lighting for night games (which significantly raised attendance at those games), artificial turf (better known as the "damn rug" or "#*&%! carpet"), domes (so games could be played during snowstorms), and ridiculous electronic scoreboards that explode or launch astronauts whenever the home team hits a home run. The consummate bluffer needs to memorize only a few ballparks (since the earlier complete list should be written on your sleeve or Scotch taped to your wrist).

Yankee Stadium in New York—better known as the "House that Ruth built." Actually, Ruth was not remembered for her construction ability and was never seen mixing cement. Known for its short right field fence (the "porch"), monuments in center field, and irate New Yorkers.

Fenway Park in Boston—remarkable for its "Green Monster." Not to be confused with the Fenway frank (the ballpark's infamous hotdog), the Green Monster is actually the left field wall just 280 feet away but a mere six feet shorter than the Empire State Building. The Monster has recently been classified as one of the eight wonders of the modern world.

Candlestick Park in San Francisco—entering players and fans are admonished to load up with heavy items in their pockets to avoid being blown into the Pacific Ocean. On a calm day at the Stick, long fly balls to deep right field are routinely snagged by the catcher.

Houston Astrodome—built in 1965, constructed to stop opposing hitters from blasting the ball out of the park.

When you refer to a stadium or ballpark, don't worry about statistics, history, or measurements. Simply say, "Let's go early to the ballyard and catch BP." Calling it a "ballyard" (as the ballplayers do) puts you in the know, and wanting to watch boring batting practice (BP) makes you a real afficionado. After that you can shut up and smile knowingly. Of course, you should know the name of the ballpark you're in if you're at a game. Or at least the city.

Expansion, Franchise Shifting, and Relocation

Expansion. Say it with a scowl on your lips. Expaaan-shun. To the baseball purist, it's the worst thing since money-grubbing owners deep-sixed double-headers. Of course, without expaaanshun, major league baseball would never have come to Texas or Georgia or Canada or California, etc., etc. Or Guam. (Not yet.) Used to be eight teams in each league, all within a train ride of each other. Easy to know most of the players. Possible to complete a set of baseball cards. Now with 12 teams in the National League and 14 in the American (figure that one out!), collecting baseball cards requires a spare room. Two hundred and fifty *more* players. Fifty or sixty *more* coaches and managers and player's agents.

For the bluffer, knowing the trail of teams is *de rigueur* ("required" for you rubes). Some are easy: the Brooklyn Dodgers became the Los Angeles Dodgers; the New York Giants became the San Francisco Giants. Some are tougher: the Boston Braves (originally the Boston Beaneaters) became the Milwaukee Braves became the Atlanta Braves. And some are downright ridiculous: the Philadelphia Athletics became the Kansas City Athletics became the Oakland Athletics became the Oakland A's became the Oakland Athletics. (Not to be confused with the Philadelphia Phillies, who never left.) Like the Oakland Athletics/A's/Athletics, a few teams didn't bother moving when things got bad; they simply changed their names. The Houston Colt .45's (an expansion team) became the Houston Astros. But typically, teams that play so poorly not only move, they *also* change their names to avoid leaving any evidence (Seattle Pilots/Milwaukee Brewers and St. Louis Browns/Baltimore Orioles). The Washington Senators were so lousy that they moved *twice* from Washington, changing their names both times—to become the Minnesota Twins in '61, and later, after stupidly returning to the scene of the crime as an expansion team, to become the Texas Rangers in '72.

Minor League Teams

Bluffing about the minor leagues is usually a safe bluff because unless someone lives in a minor league city, they'll know absolutely nothing about the minors. Even the most ardent baseball fan doesn't waste his time trying to keep up with the hundreds of insignificant minor league teams and undistinguished players. But if you do get involved in a conversation with someone who appears knowledgeable about the minors, stay calm: he's probably bluffing, too. Both of you will then have a glorious time impressing eavesdroppers.

The minor leagues, farm system, or bush league as they are often called are basically composed of four divisions: AAA ("triple A," just below the big leagues, and no relation to your automoble club), AA ("double A"), A, and Rookies. Each major league team has a network of minor league teams to help develop players for that particular franchise. Because of the tremendous number of minor league teams, it's not worthwhile to memorize a list of teams or leagues, but here are a few to toss around:

- International League
- American Association
- California League
- Pacific Coast League
- New York-Penn
- Tri-State (which three states are unimportant)
- Sally (also an old girlfriend)
- Kitty

Most of the minor league teams take on the names of their major league affiliates such as the the Kenosha Twins, the Auburn Astros, the Tacoma Tigers (who are actually not Tiger affiliates but probably didn't want to be associated with their affiliates), but there are some names that are different and impressive:

Albuquerque Dukes	Tidewater Tides
Appleton Foxes	Nashville Sounds
Buffalo Bisons	Ashville Tourists
Toledo Mud Hens	Denver Zephyrs
Calgary Cannons	Scranton/Wilkes-Barre Red Barons

When lost in a discussion about the minors, inventing names will usually do the trick, but be careful. You're better off making up names that at least sound baseballish (although the above list could make you feel that any name will do). Stay away from names of vegetables, fruits, and foods, such as the Tallahassee Tomatoes, Bakersfield Bananas, Miami Muffins, and Ann Arbor Artichokes. Some names sound too violent for baseball, such as the Boston Stranglers or Canterbury Cutthroats, more appropriate for football teams or less-violent hockey teams.

Equipment

In the beginnings of the game, a minimum of equipment was necessary: a bat and a ball. But as more and more games were delayed by everyone having to search for the lone ball hit out of play into a cornfield (or waiting for a new bat to be whittled when the original one broke), someone got the brilliant idea of supplying more than one ball and bat.

Soon after Alexander Cartwright formalized the rules, uniforms and equipment proliferated like Fourth of July fireworks. Most teams had different color socks, shirts, belts, and caps, all depending upon the position that player was playing. This also became time consuming, since whenever, say, a pitcher was moved to shortstop, he'd have to stop and change clothes. Games ran to marathon lengths, with most of the exciting action occurring in the locker rooms, out of sight of the paying customers. So this idea was finally scrapped.

Gradually, each team adopted its own colors, and all players on each team wore the same outfit (called the "uniform uniform" concept). Additional equipment soon became necessary, some to keep the player from hurting another player (batting helmets), some to keep the player from hurting himself (athletic supporters), some to protect the player from the elements (windbreakers), and some to make a fashion statement (designer sweatbands).

Thus, from the simple bat and ball evolved a mega-industry, producing baseball pants, shirts, undershirts, stirrups, sanitary socks, knee pads, sliding pads, shoes with spikes, batting helmets, batting gloves, athletic supporters, cups, weighted bats, weighted doughnuts, wrist bands, windbreakers, thumb guards, ankle supports, cocktail napkins, and a plethora of additional equipment all essential for a simple game requiring only a bat and a ball. The bluffer should know

(1) A baseball has a cushioned cork center surrounded by tightly wound yarn (99 percent virgin wool, if available, and 1 percent other fibers and preservatives), covered by horsehide (used to be cowhide before 1974, when it was lobbied against by the NBA, National Bovine Association), which is rubbed in special mud, imported from the Delaware River, before each game. (We wonder whose relative *that* franchise belongs to.) Umpires actually spend hours before each game rubbing this mud on over 60 baseballs to give the pitcher a better grip.

(2) Major league bats are made from ash trees (the trunk, not the leaves).

(3) Home uniforms are usually bright white; away uniforms are typically bad-guy gray. At one time, visiting teams were required to wear black hats and mustaches, and snicker insidiously.

(4) A major league baseball has 108 stitches.

THE PARTICIPANTS

The Players and Their Positions

Knowing a little something about each position and a few players can make the difference between people thinking you're an experienced coach or a couch potato. Remember that certain builds or body styles will often tip you off to the position a person plays. When someone says they used to play ball, by knowing what to look for, you should be able to immediately tell them what position, what year, and in what part of the country. This always impresses, and you have at least a one-out-of-nine shot on the position.

Catchers

Catchers are usually short, round, dumpy ballplayers with hairy chests. In many cases they didn't start out short or round but became that way after years of collisions at home plate. The catcher's equipment, chest protector, mask, and shin guards are often called the "Tools of Ignorance"—not because the average IQ of a major league catcher is suspect but rather because someone would have to be shy a few marbles to want to play such a dangerous position without chain mail or a Stealth bomber. It's said that insurance premiums on catchers and skydivers are now about the same since the advent of safer catching equipment.

Actually, the catcher, not the manager, is the "brains"

of the team, since he calls the pitches, aligns infielders, and is counted on to assist on crossword puzzles when the team's traveling. The catcher must have a strong arm to stop base runners from stealing and a quick wit to antagonize batters (one reason catchers wear protective equipment, since the batter's got a bat).

Experienced catchers can always be recognized by a simple handshake, as a catcher's fingers usually point in three or four different directions at the same time. They also tend to refuse chairs at the dinner table. Two catchers you should be most familiar with are

Yogi Berra – the former Yankee Hall of Famer, known for his philosophical insights, called "Yogi-isms" or "Berraisms." "The game's not over 'til it's over," "If people don't want to come out to the park, nobody's gonna stop 'em," or "Eighty percent of the game is pitching, the other half's hitting." Berra was once asked his cap size during spring training. His reply, "How do I know? I'm not in shape yet!" is still the watchword for the finely conditioned athlete.

Johnny Bench – the former Cincinnati Reds great, may be best remembered for being host of the Saturday morning pregame show called the *Baseball Bunch*. His many talents on the field may be overshadowed by the cartoons he competed with on Saturday morning.

First Basemen

First basemen are large, so that the other fielders can spot them easily from across the field. With the many people who are running toward first base – the batter, who's just hit a ground ball, the umpire, the first base coach, the NBC cameraman, the groundskeepers, the ball boys, etc.—the fielders know to throw to the big guy. This can be a problem if the NBC cameraman is also large, unless, of course he's a better fielder than the first basemen. First basemen must have sure hands because they handle so many throws and are asked on road trips to deal in card games. They must also have quick feet to deftly touch first base while catching the ball and avoiding the runner, umpire, first base coach, NBC cameraman, groundskeepers, and ball boys.

Often, great players at other positions play the twilight years of their careers at first base because it's so close to the dugout and because they can use a gigantic glove, enabling them to catch the ball without any human effort. (First basemen's gloves have been known to be used by animal hunters to catch woolly mammoths and other medium-sized beasts.) You should be familiar with the following first basemen:

Lou Gehrig—Yankee slugger and Hall of Famer, known as the "Iron Horse" because he played more consecutive games than anyone in the history of the sport—30 million or thereabouts.

John "Boog" Powell—former Oriole, Indian, and Dodger, known for his lite beer commercials and being called "Boog." Amateur genealogists suggest that at Powell's birth his dad said, "Look at that little Booger!" and it stuck. Anyone who's seen childhood photos of the Booger realizes it could have been much worse.

Dick Stuart—Pirate star known affectionately as "Dr. Strangeglove" for his many uses of his first baseman's glove, none of which included catching the ball.

Second Basemen

Second basemen are the "Mr. Average" of the infield. They are usually of medium size, medium build, and order their steaks medium. They typically wear average clothes, got average grades in school, drive average cars, and have 2.3 children. If it weren't for the fact that they must be fairly agile (walk and chew gum at the same time) to turn the double play from second to first, you might have trouble seeing the second basemen, as they blend into the grass. But there have been some real standouts:

Joe Morgan—Cincinnati star second sacker known as "Little Joe," best known for trying to fly when in the batter's box. The wind current created by the rapid flapping movement of his left arm was never enough for complete liftoff, so Little Joe decided to become the all-time home run leader for second basemen. His arm movement became known as the funky chicken and can be seen at any disco.

Rogers Hornsby—St. Louis hitting star known as the "Rajah," had the incredible batting average of .424 in 1924. Since he was also manager, he didn't have the added pressure of trying to keep his position.

Jackie Robinson—Brooklyn Dodger great, best remembered for breaking the color line in baseball but should also be remembered for playing himself in the 1951 movie called *The Jackie Robinson Story*. Critics said the actor wasn't tall enough to play the great Robinson.

Rod Carew—Minnesota Twins star, probably the least-known best hitter in baseball during his career. Some say that his outstanding batting averages year after year could be attributed to the defense having to play on an ice infield in the hinterlands of Minnesota. These critics shut up when he continued his fine hitting for the California Angels.

Nelson "Nellie" Fox – Chicago star, best known for the amount of chewing tobacco he could store in one cheek without exploding and for inventing a bat with no knob that you could hold at either end.

Third Basemen

Most third basemen are big, dull, brutish players with bruises all over their bodies. Since most batters are right handed, the bruises come from the blistering baseballs hit toward third base, hence the name "hot corner." During a game, a third baseman needs to have fast hands to protect both his interests and those of his wife. So good reflexes, nerves of steel, and adequate health coverage are key qualifications when a manager considers a potential third baseman. Wiseacres quip that a few teams considered importing sumo wrestlers to cover this dangerous position but talks broke down over a uniform dispute. The average playing life of a third basemen is fairly short, ranging from 10 minutes to about 2 years. Within a recent 10-year period, the Los Angeles Dodgers had over 60 different third basemen dodge bullets and finally surrender.

A few third basemen you should note are

Willie "Puddin' Head" Jones – Philadelphia third baseman, renowned for being called "Puddin' Head."

Brooks Robinson – Baltimore Orioles star known as the "Vacuum Cleaner" or "Hoover" for his amazing ability to field impossible ground balls and for keeping his room spotlessly clean.

Mike Schmidt – Philadelphia Phillies home run and third base fielding star, who actually lived through an amazing 18 seasons of Philadelphia pitching without a whimper.

Pie Traynor – Pirate Hall of Famer who lasted 17 years at the hot corner, often confused with a local Pittsburgh circus act featuring smart bakery goods.

George Brett – Kansas City hitting star, remembered for hitting a home run with a bat illegally drenched in a sticky substance called pine tar. The dispute arose when the bat stuck to the ball as it cleared the right field fence. Brett also received much attention when he sat out a good part of one season because of a hemorrhoid problem. Actually, "sitting out" isn't the right term.

Eddie Matthews – Milwaukee Braves slugger, known for being a Milwaukee Braves slugger.

Shortstops

The shortstop is the chatterbox of the infielders. Usually a sinewy player with catlike reflexes, he wears a 39″-long suit jacket and has a mouth that moves a mile a minute (usually shortstops, catchers, and pitchers later become announcers or used-car salesmen). A shortstop has Gumbylike qualities, making acrobatic plays from all angles. Typically, the shortstop has the most accurate arm and is the best fielder on the team, unless of course, the owner's nephew happens to be the shortstop. Shortstops seem to have an insatiable love of the game and are always ready to play. They are easily identified at social events by their knickers, sliding pads, and cleated shoes. A few shortstops every bluffer should know are

Ernie Banks—"Mr. Sunshine," Chicago Cubs star shortstop best known for his home run power, which is rare for shortstops, his soft-spoken manner, which is also rare for shortstops, and his famous line "It's a great day for a game . . . let's play two."

Maury Wills—former Dodger great, known for stealing 104 bases in one season. To slow down this amazing base stealer during a crucial series, the San Francisco Giants considered changing Candlestick Park into Candlestick Terrarium by augmenting the base paths with quicksand.

Ozzie Smith—the St. Louis Cardinal magician called the "Wizard of Oz" and known for his somersaults and other acrobatics. His positioning in the field has raised a question—should he be called a shortstop or short left fielder?

Left Fielders

Left fielders are usually tall and slow. Their galloping gait sets them apart from the other, more fleet-of-foot outfielders. Left fielders are usually outstanding hitters who can't play any other position. In Little League and other youth baseball leagues, the left fielder is your best fielder, but rarely so in the majors. A few left fielders you should be familiar with include

Ted Williams—the Boston Red Sox Hall of Famer, known as the "Splendid Splinter" and the "Kid." He was the last player to have a batting average of over .400 (.406 in 1941) and still lost in the Most Valuable Player voting to Joe DiMaggio who hit a measly .357.

Stan "the Man" Musial — St. Louis Cardinal Hall of Famer, also a fine first baseman. Musial was not your typical left fielder, since he could run like the wind. He did, however, have the first $100,000 contract — when $100,000 was actually worth $100,000.

Carl Yastrzemski — better known as "Yaz," had the unenviable job of taking over left field from Ted Williams. But rumor has it that as the son of a Long Island potato farmer who practiced hitting potatoes with a rake, he could hit anything. He was the last triple-crown winner (led the league in home runs, batting average, and runs batted in). "Yaz" could also run and field so well that now some baseball historians insist that maybe he didn't play left field.

Pete Rose — Cincinnati, Philadelphia, and Montreal star, holds too many batting records to list here. Some will say he was really a multiposition player, since he made the All-Stars at four or five different positions. We just happened to have room for him in left field. Rose, better known as "Charlie Hustle," played first base, second base, third base, outfield, and some say, the horses. Adept at every position, he was therefore one of the few stars who could throw the ball around the infield all by himself.

Joseph Jefferson "Shoeless Joe" Jackson — remembered as one of the 1919 Black Sox whose amazing fielding, hitting (lifetime batting average of .356), and running would lead you to believe he should've been a shortstop.

Left fielders also have had their share of players with unusual names and nicknames: Goose Goslin, Cool Papa Bell, and Heinie Manush (no kidding!).

Center Fielders

Center fielders are the fleet-footed greyhounds of this glamour spot in the outfield. They are dynamic and daring, exhibiting boundless energy while covering the most territory. Not unlike traveling salesmen. They are not only the fastest, but also the surest handed and best fielders. People who play the outfield will always say that they play center field, even if they don't, because they're too embarrassed to admit playing left or right field. Whatever happens, you can't hide in center field, except in Yankee Stadium where there are tall monuments. Some center field wonders every bluffer (or anyone over three years old) should know include

Mickey Mantle – Yankee slugger called the "Mick," the most prolific switch-hitter in major league history. Mick not only could hit, but also was considered one of the fastest runners in a straight line and uphill. The story goes that *"Mick* was the *Key,* the *Man* who would *Tell,"* hence *Mickey Mantle.* He was also known for losing baseballs – hitting 'em out of the ballpark. The longest home run ever measured was Mick's 565-foot blast against the Washington Senators (the ball club, not the legislators).

Willie Mays – New York and San Francisco Giant star known as the "Say Hey Kid." Mays could do it all: run, field, throw, hit, hit with power, steal, wash, dry, you name it. He was the all-around ballplayer who excited fans by running out from under his hat.

Joe DiMaggio–Yankee star probably best known for his Mr. Coffee commercials and for being married to Marilyn Monroe (who probably had better stats than Joe). DiMaggio was called the "Yankee Clipper" and "Joltin' Joe." His 56-game hitting streak is still a record. His $100,000 contract is no longer a record.

Ty Cobb–Detroit star known as the "Georgia Peach," had a reputation for being a tough competitor who would sharpen his spikes before each game. Awe-struck competitors intimated that this 12-time batting champ must have cut across the pitcher's mound, going directly from first to third while the lone umpire was watching the flight of the ball.

Duke Snider–Brooklyn Dodger known as the "Silver Fox" and the "Duke of Flatbush," not really a duke but did hit over 40 home runs five times. Unfortunately, as good as he was, he was probably only the third best center fielder in New York at that time. But being rated behind Mays and Mantle or Mantle and Mays isn't too embarrassing.

Right Fielders

Often characterized as the Paul Bunyans of the baseball world, for their size, stamina, and growths on the feet, right fielders are usually tall, strong, have 46″ chests, and are ideal dates for your single sister. While in Little League getting sent to right field is like being exiled to Siberia (and labeled worst player/all-around wimp), there's nothing wimpy about a major league right fielder. They're usually nicknamed the "Whammer," the "Slammer," the "Bammer," or "Hammerin' Hank," and you'd be crazy (or a masochist) to mock a right fielder. You should know and pay homage to these:

George Herman Ruth – better known as the "Babe," the "Bambino," or "Jidge" (mispronunciation of George) to his teammates, began as an outstanding pitcher. Someone, in his infinite wisdom, gave the Babe a bat, and the rest is history. Unfortunately for the hapless Red Sox, their owner was preoccupied with producing a Broadway show for his honey to star in. Convinced that anyone with the name of George Herman (and last name Ruth) had little chance of being a slugger, he sold Ruth to the New York Yankees so he could finance his show. Red Sox fans claim they've been cursed ever since.

Henry Aaron – "Hammerin' Hank," the star Milwaukee and Atlanta Braves right fielder who broke Ruth's all-time home run record. Quietly hitting 30 to 40 home runs each year from 1954 to 1975, Aaron amassed a total of 755 home runs and was inducted into baseball's Hall of Fame before most people realized his consistency and power. Which can happen when you spend half a brilliant career in Milwaukee.

Reggie Jackson – "Mr. October." Though he struck out more than any other man in history (2597), he's sixth in all-time home runs. As a promotion, fans were once given "Reggie" bars at a game. After Reggie walloped a home run, time had to be called to clean up the 40,000 Reggie bars tossed onto the field. There's still doubt as to whether it was a tribute to Reggie or a blunt statement about the bar's taste.

Roberto Clemente – exciting Pirate right fielder, first Hispanic to be elected to the baseball Hall of Fame.

He led the Pirates to two world championships and finished with a .317 batting average and 3000 base hits but was almost unheard of because he played his *entire* career in Pittsburgh. (Playing an *entire* career anywhere is now almost unheard of.)

Roger Maris – the "Rajah," "Mr. Flat Top." Poor Roger. He had to play in the shadow of Mickey Mantle, the popular Yankee center fielder. And he had the nerve to break Babe Ruth's record 60-home-run season. Though Maris was a consistent hitter and winner, he couldn't compete with two legends.

Pitchers

Pitchers are the matinee idols of the baseball world, often described as tall, blonde, handsome Robert Redford types who get to be in magazine underwear commercials. Whoever gave this description didn't review mug shots of some of the best known pitchers – with their ubiquitous five-o'clock shadow, surly expression, and bloodshot eyes. Because the pitcher is the focal point of the team, he must be cocky, obnoxiously self-confident, and undaunted by extreme pressure and booing fans and relatives.

Some pitchers are known for their blazing fastball, or "heater" as it's called. Others for their slider, sinker, curve, knuckler or screwball. The pitcher's selection of his pitches often reflects his personality. Any discussion of baseball will ultimately end up talking about pitchers, so you better do your homework.

Because baseball has become so specialized, there are basically four types of pitchers: (1) starting pitchers, who only start games and rarely finish (since it's not in their contracts), (2) long relievers, who come in to relieve the starting pitcher when he gets bombed in the early innings, (3) short relievers, who may be tall but pitch only the last few innings of a game because it's in their contract and they have better things to do in the first few innings, and (4) batting practice pitchers who never pitch in a game (because they have no contract) but who try to build the hitters' egos by throwing the ball so that it can be hit about 5000 feet. A good basis for a bluff starts with

Walter Johnson – legendary Hall of Famer known as the "Big Train." Hapless batters insisted that he could throw so fast that he once pitched an inning without using a baseball, and no one noticed.

Cy Young – known for an award named after him. Remember, the "Cy" stands for "Cyclone."

Christy Mathewson – an original Hall of Famer known for having the most World Series shutouts and bringing credence to the saying "You can't hit what you can't see."

Bob Feller – Cleveland fireballer, whose fastball was actually raced against a motorcycle officer to test its speed. (It got a ticket.)

Edward "Whitey" Ford – Yankee star known for his World Series records and lite beer commercials with Mantle (at least he never had to pitch to the Mick).

Sandy Koufax – Dodger Hall of Fame left hander who pitched three no-hitters and a perfect game. A strikeout artist, he once himself struck out 12 times in a row (so he knows the pain he inflicted).

Bob Gibson – St. Louis Cards star, a gifted athlete who

once played for the Harlem Globetrotters. He's the only player to ever try to slam dunk a baseball.

Leroy Robert "Satchel" Paige – legendary star from the Negro leagues who played for Cleveland, probably the oldest player to play the game. He pitched three scoreless innings for Kansas City at the ripe old age of 60 or 70 or 80; no one is quite sure. He was best known for his advice "Don't look back, something may be gaining on you," and "How old would you be if you didn't know how old you were?" It's said "Satch" pitched a series of games using a bottle cap as home plate and didn't walk a batter.

Grover Cleveland Alexander – Hall of Fame pitcher named after a president (Calvin Coolidge), who was played by a future president, Ronald Reagan, in a movie about his life – *The Winning Team,* 1952.

Don Drysdale – Dodger star known for pitching 58 scoreless innings and selling automatic pool covers. Drysdale twice hit seven home runs in a season (at that rate he would need over 100 seasons to break the most home runs by a pitcher – Babe Ruth, 714).

Nolan Ryan – "Nolie," the "Ryan Express," the ageless wonder who has the most no-hitters in major league history, had his slow ball clocked at the speed of light, and who just keeps on getting better. Unverified reports contend that a lobby group called the Professional Hitters Association has been pressuring the commissioner to install a mandatory retirement age for all pitchers from Texas.

Steve Carlton – "Lefty," star pitcher said to have stuck his hand in a barrel of rice for conditioning, starting a new exercise called riceometrics.

Warren Spahn –"Spahnie," Milwaukee Braves star whose autograph (if legible) went for $5 in 1989.

Pitchers are often known for their unique and sometimes zany nicknames: Jim "Catfish" Hunter, Mark "the Bird" Fydrich, Dennis "Oil Can" Boyd, Jay Hanna "Dizzy" Dean, Paul Dee "Daffy" Dean, Dwight "Doc" Gooden, and Van Lingle Mungo and Orel Hershiser (whose names are zany enough as they are).

If you get sucked into a discussion about left handed pitchers, refer to them as southpaws or "da lefty," since most left handed pitchers are called "Lefty" (Lefty Gomez, Lefty Grove, Lefty O'Lefty . . .).

Relief Pitchers

Relief pitchers are unusually large, sullen, evil look-ing, and mustached. They look like the bad guys in spaghetti westerns. They're referred to as the "stopper" or "fireman" and must have nerves of steel because of the situations they're dropped into. Imagine being brought into a situation with the bases loaded, no one out, tie score, bottom of the last inning, rain starting, wind blowing, hostile fans jeering, an umpire with a minuscule strike zone, and the greatest hitter in all of baseball coming to the plate. Your job is on the line! So you develop this mean, crazed, intimidating look when you step out onto the mound. Your name has to sound tough so that when the public address an-nouncer announces you as the new pitcher, the bat-ter's legs start to quiver. (Obviously, "Puddin' Head" Jones and "Scooter" Rizzuto were *not* relief pitchers.) The names and the looks that follow should be remembered by any serious bluffer.

Al "Mad Hungarian" Hrbowsky – known for his method of psyching up (eating nails or something). How'd *you* like to bat off a pitcher called the Mad Hungarian?

Rollie Fingers – Oakland A's star known for his handlebar mustache and his scowl. With his name, he would have made a great pirate in a Douglas Fairbanks film. "Aye, Aye, Captain Fingers!"

"Goose" Gossage – known for his mean look, mustache, and fireball. Rumors abound about the origin of his nickname, but we've traced it back to either the goosebumps he gave opposing hitters or the goose eggs (zero runs) opposing teams scored against him. Take your pick.

Dick "Monster Man" Radatz – Boston star known for his unusual Halloween costumes and being called "sir." (When you're 6'5", 240 pounds, people tend to call you "sir" a lot.)

Ryne Duren – Yankee fireballer known for playing up his poor eyesight and wildness. While warming up to pitch, he'd intentionally throw a pitch so wild that batters were scared to death to get into the batter's box. Because of his blazing speed as a youth, he was banned from pitching high school baseball, so he proceeded to *average* 22 strikeouts per game in an adult league. He's said to have once pitched three perfect innings to first base before being turned 90 degrees clockwise by a teammate and was rumored to have once hit three batters in one inning, two in the on-deck circle and one in the dugout.

The Bench Jockey

Most people think that there are only nine players on a baseball team, but really, one of the key players on any team sits on the bench. No, it's not the manager or star pinch hitter – it's the bench jockey. The bench jockey is a player who continually and loudly derides the opposition with disparaging, degrading, and often humorous remarks about the opposing players and their families. His ability to get under the opposition's skin is invaluable during critical times in the game. This quick-witted, sharp-tongued player needs to know just the right time to fire the zinger. Motormouth, as his teammates affectionately refer to him, starts more fights than a boxing-bell ringer but seems to never get into one. Teams have been known to pay high prices for these verbal abusers and have traded star players to attain one. No team has ever won a World Series without an all-star bench jockey. Unfortunately, we can't name any of the top bench jockeys because most of them have changed their names and been relocated with new identities somewhere in South America. But it's always good to know a couple of bench jockey zingers so you can bluff at the ballpark. Using the proper intonations and syllable emphasis is vital.

- "Ah, yah mudda wears combat boots!"
- "Wehd ya lurn ta tro da ball, in sissy school?"
- "He ain't a pitcha, e's a glassa wadda!"
- "Wehd ya find dat busher, in a tomato patch?"
- "Ya swingin like a rusty gate!"
- "Wiff da bum!"

and so on. We never said the bench jockey's barbs had any literary value.

Managers

As the saying goes, "If you win it's the players; if you lose, it's the manager." And on this philosophy has rested the fate of many a manager. Managers don't have a lot of job security. You see, if the team plays poorly, the owner can either replace the 25-man roster or fire one manager. Some decision, especially since most managers were crummy players before they became managers. As a matter of fact, managers are not only fired, but often traded to other teams, or used as change in arms-to-terrorist transactions.

Connie Mack, "Mr. Baseball," must have been a terrific manager because he spent 53 seasons! as manager of the same team, the Philadelphia Athletics — a record that will probably never be broken. Not wholly incidentally, however, he was also owner of the team. The few managers you should know include

Leo "the Lip" Durocher — remembered for his association with the Hollywood crowd and his marriage to actress Laraine Day. He loudly managed the Dodgers, Giants, Cubs, and Astros.

Miller Huggins — known as the "Mighty Mite" and the "Hug" and for being continually kidded by Babe Ruth. He managed the Cards and Yankees.

Casey Stengel — known as the "Old Perfessor" and for inventing his own language called Stengeleze. He managed the Yankees, Dodgers, Braves, and, as final punishment, the New York Mets.

Earl Weaver — known for arguing with umpires. The first manager to "double-substitute," enabling him to place his relief pitcher just about anywhere he wanted in the batting order. Managed the Orioles.

Walter Alston – quiet, unassuming manager of the Dodgers. Alston was so quiet and unassuming that he was absent for six months during the '54 season before anyone realized he was gone. Players claim that during this period his pregame pep talks were particularly inspirational.

Billy Martin – known for his exciting brand of baseball called "Billyball," his temper, his TV commercials, and for the number of times he was hired, fired, hired, fired . . . as manager of the New York Yankees by George Steinbrenner.

Owners and Execs

Owners of ball clubs come from all walks of wealthy life. Some are silent owners, some are controversial owners, some are inspirational owners, and some are innovative owners. But all are wealthy owners. Let's start with the creative geniuses, the innovators:

Bill Veeck – (pronounced like "heck" or "wreck" or "schmeck") one-time owner or exec of the St. Louis Browns, the Cleveland Indians, and the Chicago White Sox, known for being the first real baseball promoter, the P. T. Barnum of the baseball world. Among his many ingenious ideas were the exploding scoreboard with home run fireworks and the use of midget Eddie Gaedel (3'7", 65 pounds) as a pinch hitter in 1951. After popping out of a huge cake at a ceremony between games of a doubleheader, Gaedel was announced as a pinch hitter in the second game and walked on four pitches. Since that time, anyone with a strike zone smaller than the size of a baseball was banned from playing in the major leagues.

Charles O. Finley – (better known as "Charlie O") an insurance tycoon and former owner of the Oakland Athletics, another innovator. Finley was obviously a frustrated interior decorator, as he attempted to use orange baseballs and green and gold uniforms. His team mascot, a jackass kept in the bullpen, was also named Charlie O, and the two of them were often mistaken for one another in photographs. Finley actually offered his star pitcher, Vida Blue, a great sum of money to change his first name to True.

Gene Autry – owner of the California Angels, a singing cowboy, movie star, TV star, and songwriter before he became owner of the Angels. Some of his early teams would probably have been better off singing. Autry's most famous song, "Rudolph the Red-Nosed Reindeer," was written after an embarrassing defeat and subsequent night on the town.

George Steinbrenner – the only one of the many controversial owners who could dismantle a dynasty without working up a sweat. Owner and iron-fisted czar of the New York Yankees, he's probably best known for alienating players and firing managers Billy Martin, Bob Lemon, Billy Martin, Yogi Berra, Billy Martin, Lou Pinella, Billy Martin, Ralph Houk, Billy Martin, and Billy Martin.

Phil Wrigley – owner of the Chicago Cubs, known for his Juicy Fruit gum, his team that trained on Catalina island, and his ballpark (Wrigley Field) which had no lights. Wrigley's concept of playing games without lights saved him a great deal in electricity bills but made watching night games particularly difficult.

Charles Comiskey – owner of the Chicago White Sox, turned Black Sox. His many contributions to the game are overshadowed by his use of a coin changer to pay his players, many of whom were on food stamps. He is said to have contributed to the World Series scandal of 1919 when his team took a bribe and threw the series in order to make their car payments.

Branch Rickey – exec of the Browns, Cardinals, Dodgers, and Pirates. To supply his major league team with talent, Rickey was the first owner to establish his own farm system (now called a "chain gang"). Though Rickey is held in high esteem for breaking the baseball color line by hiring Jackie Robinson to play for the Brooklyn Dodgers, he was also the first owner to build sand pits for his teams to practice sliding.

Recent part-owners of major league clubs include Bing Crosby (Pittsburgh Pirates), Danny Kaye (Seattle Mariners), and Bob Hope (whose Cleveland Indians provided him with one-liners for many years).

Umpires

Every sport needs an official, some higher authority to maintain order and make vital decisions during a game. Someone who can be yelled at when there's nothing to cheer about. So the umpire was created and forced to wear black so that he could be easily identified as the bad guy. You must remember that cheering for an umpire is an instant giveaway of lack of baseball knowledge and etiquette.

Umpiring is a noble profession and, as former

National League umpire Dick Stello once said, "It's the only profession where you've got to be perfect the first day on the job, and after that show constant improvement."

As a matter of fact, there are special schools for umpires, umpire training camps, special magazines (*Referee Illustrated, Umpires Quarterly, Better Umps and Gardens*, etc.), and ear plug manufacturers.

The early umps were smarter than modern umpires, borne out by the fact that umpires in the late 1800s sat in rocking chairs 20 feet behind home plate. Not only was this safer and more relaxing, it was also conducive to milder, less emotional decisions, more stylish casual wear, more relaxed knitting, and midday naps. Modern umpires wear suits of armor, yell and scream at even the good plays, and have no sense of humor. Some famous or infamous umpires include

Ron Luciano – known for his book *The Umpire Strikes Back*, his lite beer commercials, and for his famous quote "You gotta be dumb, a masochist, or a sadist or something to be an umpire."

Cal Hubbard – Hall of Fame umpire who officiated in football and baseball without changing uniforms.

Chris Pelekoudas – known for having his name misspelled more often then any other umpire. Pelikudas served from 1960 to 1975. Pelakoodus had his best year in 1962, winning 12 arguments and losing only one.

Paul and Ed Runge – the father-son combination that made a good case for poor eyesight being hereditary.

Bill Klem – often given credit for his innovations in

travel and hotel arrangements and the separate shower and dressing room for umpires – far, far, far away from team dressing rooms.

Each umpire has his own unique method of calling strikes, balls, safe, and out. "Steeeeerike" is a commonly used method for strikes. "Baaaah" is common for ball. "Auuuurgh" is common for foul tips off the ump's shins. When talking about umpires, simply toss out the names Ed Vargo, Al Barlick, Doug Harvey, Emmet Ashford, Tom Gorman, and Jocko Conlon and remark upon their unique style of singing out third strikes. Or throw out the names of three nearsighted local baseball umps, Ron Dugar, Glenn Fajardo, and Bill Bauman, who paid us to mention their names in this book (but not enough to spell them correctly). If anyone recognizes these last three names, continue the conversation, they *must* be bluffing.

And finally, two things to remember:

(1) Don't brag to anyone that you collect umpire cards or have an autographed pair of glasses from an umpire, even if you do.
(2) To tell the difference between an American League ump and a National League ump, remember, AL umps now wear red blazers, and NL umps wear blue blazers. If you're really sharp, you can tell anyway by which teams are playing.

Announcers

Few baseball discussions stay focused on the game itself, but rather delve into the really important parts of the sport, the periphery. Knowing a few baseball announcers will prove helpful should talk somehow get around to television and radio. Some announcers are former baseball stars who have loads of baseball insight, some are ardent baseball followers who have migrated from other sports or game shows with lots of enthusiasm, and some are former managers who really know nothing about the game and should have migrated to another country. You should know

Mel Allen – former NY Yankee announcer, his southern drawl popularized the home run call "Going, going, gone!" And so was Allen when the Yanks fell into the cellar and restructured their entire organization. He now announces *This Week in Baseball*.

Vin Scully – the popular red-headed Dodger announcer who's announced all kinds of sports for Saturday's NBC television specials. His 82-hour, play-by-play account of the Spasky-Fischer chess match was particularly exciting.

Harry Caray – venerable announcer for the Cardinals, White Sox, and Cubs, known for leading the crowd in "Take Me Out to the Ball Game" during the seventh-inning stretch. Speculation that he was a Japanese fighter pilot in World War II is without foundation.

Bob Uecker – "Mr. Passed Ball," known for his lite beer commercials and ability to turn an undistinguished baseball career into an equally undistinguished Hollywood career.

Joe Garagiola – former game show host, former regular on NBC's *Today* show, former boyhood friend of Yogi Berra, and, some people maintain, former St. Louis Cardinal catcher.

RULES AND LANGUAGE

The Rules

Some people contend that rules are meant to be broken, but in baseball, rules are meant to be changed. Since the mid 1800s, when it took nine balls to walk a batter and four strikes for a strikeout (and a strike was called even if the ball bounced over the plate), the rules have evolved and evolved and evolved to today's fine-tuned regulations. Cynics speculate that the number of strikes for a strikeout was changed from four to three to fit the lyrics of the song "Take Me Out to the Ball Game." ("And it's one, two, three strikes you're out at the old ball game.")

Since rule changes are as pervasive as bumper stickers, try to become familiar with these important few before someone fiddles with them again:

Rule 5.06—When a batter becomes a runner and touches all bases legally, he shall score one run for his team. (Hard as it may be to believe, this is probably the only rule that hasn't been changed yet, but we're waiting.)

The Infield-Fly Rule—Has nothing to do with the use of insect repellent on the playing field nor with the shortstop's desire for a zipper instead of buttons on his uniform pants.

The DH Rule—In the American League, a pitcher

doesn't get to bat; a "designated hitter" (DH) subs for him. In the National League too, pitchers don't hit; instead of using a DH, they stand at the plate and weakly wave their bats at the ball three times. Purists say that the American League DH Rule eliminates strategy. (Should the pitcher bunt? Should he be replaced with a pinch hitter? Should he sell his bonds and buy mutual funds?) But most say the rule eliminates their only chance to go get a hotdog.

The 210-Foot Fence Rule – In 1884, the National League made 210 feet the minimum distance for an outfield fence. Since the Chicago White Stockings' fence was just 196 feet from home plate, balls hit over it then became ground-rule doubles. Not coincidentally, the formerly slugging White Stockings soon become known as the "hitless wonders."

The 325-Foot Fence Rule – Rule 1.04 stipulates that all fields built after 1958 must have a minimum distance of 325 feet from home plate to the nearest fence and 400 feet from home to center. The Red Sox (with their 280 foot left-field wall) decide not to relocate to Allston.

In baseball, there are rules about everything: size of bases, size of gloves, size of shoes, distance to bases, distance to fences, how to get to bases, how to get to fences, fielding, pitching, batting, running, throwing, chewing, eating, and swallowing. Be keenly aware of the hand movements of your bluffee during a rules discussion to make sure he's not reaching into a vest pocket for a rule book—or a gun. These discussions are usually anxiety filled.

Lingo

When referring to certain plays, the real fan *never* uses common baseball terms. Rather, the ballyard-wise nonchalantly refer to the most normal, dull baseball moments with exciting, colorful jargon. If you want to sound in the know, memorize these terms:

DON'T SAY	INSTEAD, SAY
home run	dinger, round tripper, four bagger, tater
runners on every base	bases loaded, bags filled
bases-loaded home run	grand slam
triple or three-base hit	three bagger
double	two bagger
single	bingle, one bagger
strike out	whiff, fan, punched out, "K" (last letter of the word "struck")
base	bag, sack
home plate	platter, dish
line-drive hit	rope, frozen rope, trolley line, screamer, rocket, shot
bloop hit just out of reach of the infielder	Texas leaguer, tweener, squib
third base	hot corner
baseball	pill, apple, horsehide
bat	stick, club, toothpick, lumber, ax
pitcher	hurler, ace, chucker
pitcher and catcher	battery
lousy pitcher and crummy catcher	dead battery

relief pitcher	fireman
bean ball	duster, chin music
fast runner	"He's got wheels!"
fastball pitcher	"He can bring it!" "He can sure throw heat!"
pitch hit for a home run	gopher ball ("It'll 'gopher' a home run.")
next batter up	on deck
left handed pitcher	southpaw, lefty, crooked arm
pitcher who throws slow stuff (knuckle-balls, change-ups)	junkman
ball hit deep to the shortstop's right	in the hole
clouds in the sky	puffs of heaven, angels
inning	stanza, frame
bruise from sliding	raspberry, strawberry, pain in the . . .
batted ball that takes a high hop over the infielder's head	Baltimore chop
baseball park	yard, ballyard
baseball infield	diamond
player who plays many positions	utility player, or jock of all trades
player in dugout who razzes the other team	bench jockey
player in dugout with poison ivy	jockey itch
substitute who rarely gets into a game	bench warmer
baseball fight or melee	rhubarb

weak throwing arm	rag arm
resilient or durable throwing arm	rubber arm
strong throwing arm	rifle, cannon
singles hitter	banjo hitter
ritual of throwing the ball around the infield or a double play from third to second to first base	around the horn
scout	bird dog
where relief pitchers warm up	bullpen
men on base	ducks on the pond
batter's stance with front foot stepping away from the plate	foot in the bucket
groundskeeper	manicurist
player who shows off a lot	hotdog
hotdog (food)	(team name) Dog, such as Dodger Dog, Astro Dog, Fenway Frank, Wrigley Wiener

Aphorisms

Unlike Berraisms, which were coined by Yogi Berra and lack redeeming social value, aphorisms are the essential sayings of baseball, the proverbs of the ball-yard, as collected and annotated by Irving R. Aphor.

• "Nice guys finish last!" Coined by loud-mouthed

manager Leo Durocher while at home shellacking a mahogany end table.

- "Take two and hit to right." Credited to the White Sox team physician—actually misquoted from "Take two (aspirin) and call me tonight."

- "Spahn, Sain, and pray for rain." The unspoken pitching strategy of the 1940s Boston Braves, whose starting rotation consisted of only two excellent pitchers (Warren Spahn and Johnny Sain) and three folding chairs. A later version in the 50s—"Spahn, Burdette, and two days of wet."

- "Wait till next year!" Brooklyn Dodger fans' perennially hopeful incantation originally attributed to General George Custer at Little Big Horn.

- "Hit 'em where they ain't!" This profound strategy, credited to Wee Willie Keeler, resulted in one player's hitting 47 consecutive foul balls.

- "Good field, no hit." Phrase stolen from playboy pitcher Bo Belinsky's little black date book.

- "First in war, first in peace, but last in the American League." The slogan for the Washington Senators.

- "I'd rather be lucky than good." Lefty Gomez's famous remark (said to have been stolen from the National Russian Roulette Team).

- "Every baseball team could use a player who plays every position superbly, never strikes out, and never makes an error—but there's no way to make him lay down his hotdog and come down out of the grandstand." Joe DeAugustine, one of the founders of Boy's Baseball, Inc., of Fontana.

Scorekeeping and Scorekeepers

Official scorekeepers are the certified public accountants of the baseball world – with the almost impossible task of keeping track of, recording, and in some cases passing judgment on every action on the field.

You've probably never heard of anyone who can name one official scorekeeper in the major (or for that matter, minor) leagues. These unsung heroes don't get no respect. Fans remember the date, day, time, place, opposing team, starting lineups, umpires, singer of the National Anthem, and batboys when Yankee pitcher Don Larsen pitched his perfect game (no runs, no hits, no errors, no one reached first base) in the 1956 World Series. But not one remembers the name of the guy who recorded that historic occasion – the official scorekeeper. One mistake by this unnamed chronicler and Larsen's historic game becomes a ho-hum one-hitter.

When Hank Aaron hit his 715th home run to break the home run record of the great Babe Ruth, Aaron was immortalized, the pitcher who was dumb enough to actually throw the pitch within Aaron's reach was immortalized, the 14-year-old boy who recovered the ball was made wealthy and now lives in Scarsdale off his investments, but not one iota of thanks was given to the scorekeeper (who could have ruled it a single and three-base error, even though it was hit over the fence).

Since the history of scorekeeping would probably be just as exciting as the history of accounting, those 324 insightfully written pages have been deleted from this guide. Instead, we jump straight into a capsule course on how to keep score.

Keeping Score

Although scoring symbols may appear at first glance like a foreign language, once you've mastered the system, it's like riding a bicycle without the saddle sores. Once you learn, you never forget, to some people's chagrin.

Many fans keep score at ballgames by filling out the score cards provided in the overpriced programs they grab on their way into the ballpark. The gentlemen yelling, "Get your scorecard, souvenirs, hats, pennants, slightly used watches . . ." is the one to look for. Another favorite line is "You can't tell the players without a score card," which, if your team is in a slump, sounds like a swell idea. Besides, you may not want to be too familiar with any names, since they'll be playing for Tacoma or Albuquerque in a matter of weeks.

Filling out the score card will help you keep track of the game. If you do it right, it'll show you the lineup, what a batter did in each inning, how runs were scored, how many errors both team committed, and whether you put too much mustard on your hotdog.

There are a number of different score sheets and ways to keep score. The two basic kinds of sheets are

Notice that one kind shows little baseball diamonds; the other shows little blank spaces. Usually an official scorebook will have the baseball diamonds, and the

programs will use the empty box format. If you're using the empty box format, simply draw the parts of the diamond as you need them. Here's a basic explanation of how to score.

Each position is given a number.

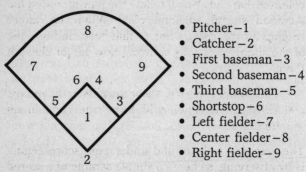

- Pitcher – 1
- Catcher – 2
- First baseman – 3
- Second baseman – 4
- Third baseman – 5
- Shortstop – 6
- Left fielder – 7
- Center fielder – 8
- Right fielder – 9

These numbers don't change with a player's ability, and you aren't supposed to use fractions, decimals, percents, or negative numbers, although 00 has shown up on occasion and $ even more recently.

The basic symbols are

1B	Single	BB	King (blues guitarist)
2B	Double	CS	Caught stealing
3B	Triple	CC	Caught cheating
HR	Home run	PO	Pick-off
E	Error	BO	Wearing dirty uniform
FC	Fielder's choice	WP	Wild pitch
HP	Hit by pitch	PB	Passed ball
BB	Base on balls	BK	Balk
IW	Intentional walk	K	Strikeout
SAC	Sacrifice	DP	Double play

SWAK	Sealed with a kiss	U	Unassisted ground out
SB	Stolen base	FO	Fly out
RB	Returned base	FI	Fly in from the coast

Across from each batter is a row of boxes to show what he did each inning. The innings are indicated by the columns. Basically, you'll follow the player around the diamond, starting at home plate. When the runner reaches a base, draw a line to that base, and use one of the simple notations showing how he (or she) got there.

- Circled numbers will show the outs in the inning.
- Filled-in diamonds will show the runs in an inning.

The best way to learn and understand scorekeeping is by observing, so here's a simple sample of a scored half inning. The Phoenix Phrogs are the visiting team, so they bat first.

	1	2
Jones	6-3 ①	
Filmore	F-8 ②	
Smeal	◇ 1B	
Rigor	◇ 2B	
Mortis	K ③	
Schmickle		
Ferd		

- Jones leads off the first inning by hitting a ground ball to the shortstop and being thrown out at first base. Score the play 6-3 (shortstop to first base), and put a circled 1 in the corner for the first out.
- Filmore hits a fly ball to the center fielder, who makes the catch for the second out. Score the play F-8 (fly out to the center fielder) and put a circled 2 in the corner for the second out.
- Smeal gets a single. Draw a line from home to first base, and put 1B under the line for single.
- Rigor hits a double. Draw a line from home to first base and from first base to second base. Put a 2B under the first line for double. Go to Smeal's box and move him (draw a line) to second base and then to third base.
- Mortis strikes out for the third out of the inning. Put a K in the box and a circled 3 for the third out. Put a slash mark at the corner of the box as a reminder to move to the next inning.

The totals for that half inning are no runs, 2 hits, no errors, and two men left on base. Go get a hotdog. Now the home team, the Denver Doughnuts, are up to bat. Since you're waiting in a long line to buy a hotdog, you give up scorekeeping for the day. Get the idea?

You may notice that many official scorebooks will have some of the abbreviations in the boxes for you to circle. If the scorecard you're using has blank boxes, then you'll have to draw the diamonds and put in the abbreviations as you go. Or make up new abbreviations.

Statistics and Figures

Baseball's a game of statistics and any knowledgeable fan will have a few up his sleeve (literally or figuratively). So here are a few to get you started:

- Almost half of all batted balls are grounders. If you hit a ground ball, you'll be out approximately 75 percent of the time. This statistic goes down the tubes if you're playing on artificial grass, then you'll probably never see the ball come down after the first bounce.
- Approximately a quarter of batted balls are fly balls. If you hit a fly ball, you'll be out about 80 percent of the time. Unless you're playing in Candlestick Park; then you'll never be put out.
- Approximately 20 percent of batted balls are line drives. If you hit a line drive, you'll be out only 30 percent of the time. If you hit a lot of these, you become a superstar and get lucrative athlete's foot spray commercials.
- Almost 10 percent of the batted balls are pop-ups. Less than one out of 13 pop-ups goes for a base hit. Unless you're playing in Candlestick Park; then you lead the league in batting.
- The distance from home plate to the pitcher's rubber is 60'6". When you're batting against Nolan Ryan or Sandy Koufax, it seems like 6'6".
- The actual distance from one base to the next is 90 feet. As you get older, the distance becomes 100 feet, 120 feet, 200 feet, and so on.
- A batting average of over .300 (30 percent success) is outstanding, and if it's done consistently over many seasons, it usually qualifies a player for the

Hall of Fame. A batting average of over .400 in any season is nearly impossible (hasn't been done since 1948 when Ted Williams hit .406). The difference between being a batting star and a bum is about four more hits a month.

- Hitting over 30 home runs in one season is very good. Hitting over 40 homers in a season is outstanding. Hitting over 50 home runs is almost unheard of. The modern record is 61 home runs by Roger Maris in 1961 ("61 in '61"). Babe Ruth held the record of 60 for many, many, many years. By the way, if you hit over 50 home runs, you're allowed to strike out in all of your other at bats and you'll still get a pay raise for next season.

- A pitcher who wins 20 games in a season is outstanding (unless he loses 40 games the same season).

- A pitcher who can throw over 90 mph is considered fast.

- A pitcher who can throw over 100 mph is considered dangerous.

- Over $50,000 in commercial endorsements per season is excellent and not unusual. Over $1,000,000 per season is not unheard of but usually results in an IRS audit and embezzlement by the player's financial manager.

SPECIAL EVENTS, MOMENTS, AND PLACES

World Series

Everyone needs a goal in life. The World Series was created to give each player such a goal. The Fall Classic comes at the end of the season and its winning team is declared the World Champions. Football fans think that the people in charge didn't know how or when to end the baseball season, so they created the World Series to guarantee a break in the action and keep the season from running from February through December. Regardless, the World Series has given every entrepreneur a chance to sell World Series memorabilia and reach his or her own financial goal.

This best-of-seven series between the champs (pennant winners) of the American League and the National League is unequaled in its importance to the civilized world. During the World Series, all other news is incidental or rescheduled, including presidential debates, elections, surprise invasions, and world wars.

There are a few key World Series events that every bluffer should be able to trot out at the crack of a bat.

- Yankee hurler Don Larsen's perfect game in 1956. Yanks vs. Bums. What's little known is that home plate umpire Babe Pinelli retired immediately after calling the final strike against pinch hitter

Dale Mitchell. Pinelli was in tears—no doubt due to the magnificent display of hitting never seen.

- Pirate second baseman Bill Mazeroski's series-winning home run in the bottom of the ninth. Pirates vs. Yanks, 1960. The Yankees outscored the Pirates 55–27 in the Series as a whole and tried to have the rules changed so total runs scored determined world champs.

- Babe Ruth's "called shot" home run in the 1932 World Series. Yanks vs. who cares? Ruth wasn't actually pointing but checking a hangnail before he stepped into the batter's box.

- Miracle Mets' World Series win in 1969 vs. the Birds. Considering the Mets' 1968 record, the miracle was that the Commissioner let them play in 1969.

- In 1920, Bill Wambsganss made the only un-assisted triple play in a World Series. It helped the Cleveland Indians beat the Brooklyn Robins. So what?

- The 1988 World Series pinch-hit home run in the bottom of the ninth inning with two outs and a full count, slugged by injured Dodger pinch hit-ter Kirk Gibson, who was so badly hobbled that he was in traction in the training room when he was called to bat. This was his only appearance in the series, as they had difficulty getting the gurney into the batter's box. If this happened in a movie, you still wouldn't believe it.

- In 1904 John McGraw's Giants refused to play in the Series—the ultimate in "If you won't play by my rules, I'm taking my ball and going home."

All-Star Game

Each year major league baseball takes time out in early July (about the middle of the season) to play an exhibition game with baseball's finest players. This is so fans (at about $50,000 per ticket) can see how the game is actually meant to be played. The All-Star Game honors baseball's stars and uses its ticket proceeds for the Baseball Player's Pension Fund so that players earning a mere million each season don't have to worry about their retirement.

Selection of the two All-Star teams (one from the National League and one from the American League) has changed over the years. At one time, the players voted for the best of their peers; at another time, the sports media; at other times, the team managers. At present, the fans choose the stars, making the All-Star Game a popularity contest of favorites (or whoever has the most relatives) rather than a contest between baseball's finest players. Last year, Meryl Streep played third base for the Nationals and went 3 for 4.

For a short time (1959–62), two All-Star Games per year were played, as if one weren't enough. The story's been bandied about that plans for 162 All-Star Games are on the drawing board, with the regular season to be eliminated altogether.

The compleat bluffer needs to know only a few important All-Star Game facts. Remarking that Carl Hubbell struck out five straight future Hall of Famers (Ruth, Gehrig, Foxx, Simmons, and Cronin) in 1934 is passé, unless, of course, you imply that you were there. Better to mention the 1961 contest held in San Francisco's windswept Candlestick Park. National League reliever Stu Miller made the first balk of his long career when he was blown off the mound in the middle of his windup. He was later recovered from the bay in the eighth inning.

Hall of Fame

The Baseball Hall of Fame is located in Cooperstown, New York, although no one is quite sure why. Abner Doubleday supposedly invented baseball in 1839 in a pumpkin patch in Cooperstown. Since Doubleday was off fighting a war when they claimed he was inventing baseball, there's a major credibility gap here, and so most scholars believe that the Hall of Fame was built in Cooperstown by mistake. Of course, many scholars also think that Shakespeare was actually Bacon. Whatever, the Hall of Fame was designed to give special recognition to the greatest of the great. Members of the Hall of Fame include players, managers, executives, umpires, and announcers, each voted in by sportswriters from every major league city.

A person becomes eligible for the Hall of Fame only after he's been retired from baseball for five years. Each Hall of Famer is represented in the gallery by a bronze plaque with a picture that bears little likeness to the honoree (not unlike a driver's license photo). Fortunately, the name, nickname, and a brief description of the person's accomplishments are also listed so that those so honored can locate their plaques. There's no greater honor in baseball than being voted a member of the Hall of Fame, except perhaps getting a candy bar named after you ("Baby Ruth," "Reggie Bar," "Milk Duds"). Hardly anyone traveling through Cooperstown fails to visit the Baseball Hall of Fame, not only because it's baseball's tribute to its great heroes, but also because it houses the only clean public restroom within two hundred miles.

Most Memorable Moments

The bluffer needs to know only a few of baseball's memorable moments, which are not necessarily super-events but sometimes obscure incidents, the recollection of which will help cement your standing as a true baseball fan. If the great moment was fairly recent, it's particularly impressive to casually imply that you were there. If it happened before you were born, you may want to reassess your "first-person" account.

Recent memorable moments at which you were "two rows behind the home dugout":

- "I'll never forget the look on Larsen's face after his perfect game ['56 Series]. Was his curve working that day or what?"
- "Nearly caught Hank Aaron's 715th dinger, but this big meathead dove in front of me . . ."
- "How about that day Bobby Thompson hit the shot heard around the world to win it for the Jints! [1951 home run to win the pennant for the Giants over the Dodgers] Spent all night listening to Branca bawling in his beer over at Morey's."
- "Talk about bum luck! Haddix pitches a perfect game for 12 innings and loses! Couldn't help but feel for the guy . . ." (1959)
- "Seems like only yesterday when Joltin' Joe kept

that 56-game streak alive [1941]. Traveled the circuit with him from the forty-fourth game on . . ."

- "Remember when the Splinter [Ted Williams] had those six hits on the final day [1941] to finish over .400? Talk about clutch hitting!"

After making one of these outlandish, conversation-stopping statements, immediately excuse yourself to the restroom so that no follow-up questions are asked. Don't return for several hours. Claim kidney problems.

Superstitions

Any overview of baseball wouldn't be complete without a thorough, detailed chapter on superstitions, an intrinsic part of the great game. Even the greenest rookie knows that merely muttering the words "no-hitter" will doom their pitcher's perfect performance and nix their team's chances of whitewashing the opposition. Stories are legion of dire consequences befalling those who step on the foul line when running out to or in from the field. Washing a favorite sweaty undershirt worn during a hitting streak will, without doubt, plunge a once-hot batter into a month-long slump. Entire teams turn their hats inside out ("rally caps") to successfully spark a late-inning comeback. And wearing garlic, rubbing bats with chicken bones, and showering in full uniform, spikes included, have helped many a star achieve Hall of Famedom. But perhaps the most long-held baseball superstition is that actually acknowledging the power of superstitions (talking or writing about same) will bring about a career batting average of .025 and a lifetime of prostate problems and all-around lousy luck. Which for good reason herewith ends our thorough, detailed discussion of superstitions.

Memorabilia

The growth of professional baseball has helped launch not only a lucrative business in athletic sportswear and sporting goods, but also an entire cottage industry of baseball memorabilia. Insignificant keepsakes such as World Series ticket stubs, penny baseball cards, and hastily scrawled autographs on the backs of soiled programs have recently enjoyed resurgent popularity, as have women's shoulder pads. But, unlike shoulder pads, baseball memorabilia have also soared in value. While the intrinsic worth of a cardboard bubble-gum card is probably less than .00003 cents, nevertheless, the demand for items even remotely associated with baseball has catapulted the baseball card into the investment domain. The investment potential of ballplayers' cards is charted daily on Wall Street, and an 0-for-5 game or a mild hitting slump has been known to send a few speculators hurtling out their tenth-story windows. Well-meaning mothers, cleaning their child's cluttered closet, have tossed shoeboxes full of gold (complete sets of 1950s, 1960s, or 1970s baseball cards) into the trash, thereby eliminating thousands of future millionaires.

When bluffing memorabilia, mention anything with even a remote connection to either Ty Cobb, Mickey Mantle, or the Brooklyn Dodgers. For example,

- "We just took out a second mortgage and bought

Mickey Mantle's nephew's third-grade report card . . ."

- "Flew to Atlantic City for the 'National' [baseball memorabilia's annual show] and managed to pick up a matchbook cover with Ty Cobb's name written on it. Well, it's kinda hard to read, so it was either Ty Cobb or Jeff Thorberg. We're not sure *who* actually signed it, but at two grand it's still a steal!"

- "I still have the strip of used adhesive tape I found outside the Brooklyn Dodger locker room in '55. Was offered twenty-eight hundred for it, but I'm no dummy . . ."

Never tangle with a memorabilia collector. Make your comment quick and get the heck out. Feign a nosebleed if necessary, as these baseball groupies eat, sleep, and drink baseball.

Baseball and the Arts

There have been countless books, poems, and songs written about the great game. Hundreds of baseball movies have been produced. To make sure that you sound in the know, here are a few essentials:

Songs and Ditties

Know the first few lines to that American classic "Take Me Out to the Ball Game" (you can mumble the rest). It's always sung during the seventh-inning stretch.

Take me out to the ball game,
Take me out with the crowd.
Buy me some peanuts and cracker-jack—

La da da da da la da da da.
And it's la da da da da da da,
Da da da da da daaaaaah.
For it's one, two, three strikes you're out
At the o-o-o-old b-a-a-a-a-ll g-a-a-a-m-e.

The "Star Spangled Banner" is always sung before a game. Since a local luminary usually leads it, you don't need to know the words, just the name and sexual peccadillos of the celeb. Contrary to popular belief, the last two words of the national anthem are not "Play ball!" They sing the Canadian national anthem in Montreal and Toronto, the words of which are best known to ice-hockey fans and whalers.

And you can't be a card-carrying fan without knowing the famous Abbott and Costello comedy bit "Who's on First?" This wonderfully confusing routine was performed on radio, television, and in the movies. Unfortunately, since we still haven't figured out who *is* on first, we can't clue *you* in. But, if you've backed yourself into a verbal corner in a baseball discussion and you need to change the subject posthaste, toss in "Who's on First?"

Poetry

Two poems that distinguish bluffers from *bluffers* are "Casey at the Bat" by Ernest L. Thayer and the more arcane "Tinker to Evers to Chance" by Franklin P. Adams. You again should know the first line or two of "Casey at the Bat" and that he strikes out to end the game.

The outlook wasn't brilliant for the Mudville Nine
    that day;

The score stood two to four with but one inning left
   to play.
Tadatadatada . . .
                           . . . mighty Casey has struck out.

Knowing a few lines of the short poem about the
most feared double-play combination of the early
1900s (Joe Tinker, Johnny Evers, Frank Chance) will
impress almost anyone:

These are the saddest of possible words:
"Tinker to Evers to Chance."

Trio of bear Cubs fleeter than birds,
Tinker to Evers to Chance.

Ruthlessly pricking our gonfalon bubble,
Making a Giant hit into a double—
Words that are heavy with nothing but trouble:
"Tinker to Evers to Chance."

Films and Movies

When it comes to movies, selecting the impressive
ones becomes more difficult. Probably the best known
(not counting the recent deluge of baseball films) are

Damn Yankees—1958, starring Tab Hunter, Gwen
   Verdon, Ray Walston, based on the hit Broadway
   musical, which was based on the hit 1939 opera *The
   Devil and Daniel Webster*, which was based on *Faust*,
   the hit 1808 play by Johann Wolfgang von Goethe
   (who pitched briefly for the Berlin Binglehoffs).

The Pride of the Yankees—1942, about Lou Gehrig,

starring Gary Cooper and in which Babe Ruth plays himself but not well (poor casting).

The Natural – 1984, starring Robert Redford as Wonderboy. Includes a brilliant display of the damage a baseball can do to a lighting fixture.

As these are the most well-known and watched films, don't bother commenting on them, as everyone has no doubt seen them. Popular recent films include:

Bull Durham – 1988, starring Kevin Costner, Susan Sarandon.
Field of Dreams – 1989, starring Kevin Costner.
Eight Men Out – 1988, not starring Kevin Costner.
Major League – 1989, probably starring Kevin Costner.

Words of Wisdom

Well, you've made it to the end and probably noticed that in many situations we recommend firing off your bluff and then feigning illness, nosebleed, hernia, etc., and leaving quickly or mumbling a lot. But these are last-resort methods of escaping and/or confusing the opposition. Think about it: if you've actually read through this guide, you have enough vital trivia to bluff with the best of them!

And finally, when you go out for that first bluff on the road to bluffing success, keep in mind the immortal words of *Saturday Night Live* baseball legend Chico Escuela, "Bazebol bin bery bery gud to me!" And if you bought this book, "Bazebol bin bery bery gud to us too!" Even if we didn't make the Little League All-Stars.

Get Bluffer's Guides at your bookstore or use this order form to send for the copies you want. Send it with your check or money order to:

Centennial Press
Box 82087
Lincoln, NE 68501

Title	Quantity	$3.95 Each
Total Enclosed		

Name_____

Address_____

City _____

State_____ Zip_____